RETURN

It was one of the phantom steeds,
for now I dream again and again
of great bay horses that Texas breeds
And of the past, dulling present pain.

I'm old, but I hear the song of the West,
Hear the horses' hooves a-flying,
Think of the cowboys gone to rest
Where the winds of Texas are sighing.
Not again the desert blooms will I see
Nor the milling herds with ivory horn
Nor ride again the land where I was born.
I loved the tune of an old guitar
the only sound of the night
save the call of herds from afar,
Where the stars were our only light.

The phantom horse has fled, now I can see
Beyond the clouds of desert sand!
The pain has gone - I'm young and free
I'll mount and ride again - my Texan land.

Anna Punshon

CASTLE POINT

Our town she stands on the Essex coast,
by the River Thames,

In days gone by Roman soldiers made their camp
on Canvey Island, which is joined to the
mainland by two roads,

There's Benfleet Creek where the Vikings
made a wooden fort.

The Battle of Benfleet fought in eight hundred
and ninety four, when King Alfred sent
his son and men at arms to wipe the
Vikings out

Viking boats were burnt in Benfleet Creek to ensure
that no-one got away.

Hadleigh Castle stands in ruins on the hill,
looking out to sea, where King Henry VIII and his
Queens would stay in days gone by.
Constable visited the site and painted the
splendid view.

The church of St James the less, stands in
Hadleigh High Street, built in the reign of
King Stephen.

General Booth set up the Salvation Army farm
on Hadleigh Downs to give the poor a chance,
and the farm is still in use today.

Mobil oil refinery stands by the River Thames
providing employment, but remains a risk on our
Eastern Coast.

Gerald Frederick Snook

A DREAM OF CHILDHOOD FANCIES

I, a lonely, forlorn mortal stood,
  In a lovely Essex wood;
Above me swayed the mighty trees,
  While gently around me . . . busy . . . some early bees;
And . . . seemly, 'Whisperings' caught my ear.

On mossy patch I sat me down,
  Among bracken richly brown,
My thoughts took flight as I gazed around,
  And once again my childhood found . . .
    To imagine the 'wee folk' near.

There swinging on Blue-bell stems,
  With shining faces like precious gems;
Imps and Pixies, the wee bells rang,
  While Gnomes and Fairies sang and sang . . .
But . . . 'Only for those who would hear.'

They scampered and made bright Fairy rings,
  Happily dancing and floating as on wings
In and out primroses and violets there,
  Not seeming to know such a thing as . . . care,
    Nor could they shed a tear.

A shadow then o'ercasts the sun,
  The dancing stops . . . away they run,
Once again all is still . . .
  Flights of fancy gone at will . . .
Nor will the 'wee folk' again appear.

Alas! Alone! Would that I could turn 'The page
  Of life' and return to a younger age dream,
  'Ere one becomes as 'Flotsam' in the years between,
    With only memory now to hold dear.

Time and time again I'll return to that wood,
  For 'tis only there can I find the good . . .
And dearest dreams once I had,
  Forgetting the hurts and sorrows that's still bad,
    And so continues year by year.

Daisie Cecil-Clarke

THE MAGPIE

A cheeky little chappie
Causing quite a stir,
Stealing if he gets the chance.
He stole my heart a while ago,
His plumage I adore.
He does not know, he does not care
About the way I feel.
Just vainly goes along his way.
Who knows what next he'll steal.

P A Lucas

THE DANCER

The dancer is the dreamer,
He dances to his own tune
The music of the soul,
He dreams of dreams a dance so real,
It entwines of what will be,
Living a life of music,
The dancer dreams.

The dreamer dances,
Making what will be will be.
Making illusion reality,
Playing a tune for all.

Follow the dancer,
The dreamer
The tune,
Follow your own dance
A dance of your own.

Peter John Altoft

MY FEELINGS

To live in England now is a sin
Why don't our English people ever win?
People from other countries you see
Get all our benefits that belong to you and me
Why don't we stand up for our rights?
Before it's too late to lose our sight
We need a new system we've had enough
Let them other people have some of the rough
They had it too good for far too long
Stand up and be counted for once be strong
These people live in houses for which we pay
While half our own people have nowhere to stay
Can you honestly tell me but don't take too long
Oh for goodness sake wake up you know it's all wrong.

V W

THE VOWS

I hate the way we quarrel and fight
I love you, seems to make it right
Will those words always save
The vows in church which we gave

I wonder will this love survive
It has so much on which to thrive
For coming soon is the stork
Surely things have got to work

A joy unlike we've ever known
A baby girl with eyes so brown
To make us see the love we feel
Like parents with a bond to seal

The love we feel makes us proud
We, are now a special crowd
The three of us forever more
Even better than the years before

J Aldred

THE RETURN OF THE SKYLARK

The little bird winging its way to
Heaven beyond the Sun
Its lungs bursting with joys to come
Awakening the hearts and minds of everyone
Those who are burdened, weary and forsaken
Wake up, wake up, follow me beyond the Sun
There is a place, not for a few, but everyone
Bless the day when we shall seek and find
the glory and the everlasting Peace to come
Follow me, follow me, beyond the Sun
I will lead the way to joys to come
Follow me, lest you forget and lose your way
Follow me everyone
'The Skylark' sweetly sang come, come
Follow me, follow me, beyond the sun.

Dorothy F White

MEMORIES

She sits by the fire, her eyes old and dim.
She can't see his picture, but she remembers him.
A young man so handsome, she fell for his charms.
She remembers the nights she spent wrapped in his arms.

She knows that he loved her, he often told her so.
Then why did he leave her, oh why did he go?
She remembers the train, as it rushed him away,
Her heart is still crying, she still hurts today.

The war was so cruel, to her it seemed a sin,
She sits by the fire and she remembers him.
Her face is quite peaceful with the hint of a smile,
Perhaps yes perhaps in a very short while,

That soldier so handsome, and so full of charms.
Will hold her forever, wrapped up in his arms.
She sleeps by the fire, the flames have grown dim
But clear are her memories, her memories of him.

M E Blunt

AGAMEMNON'S RETURN

Sleep under your stone hill-
they have robbed your gold
all the bees are fled
from your stone hive.
Down beyond Tiryns
your sail flashed on the sea,
you trudged
burdened with time and plunder
up this last hill
knowing they meant you evil
knowing the purple
spread under your feet
dared you usurp a claim
why did you tread?
Ten years away-
your eyes less keen
young lions over your gates
your trust misplaced -
don't wake -
your time was golden,
ours is the age of iron
and all the songs are dead.

Lalage Pulvertaft

CHILDREN OF THE EARTH

We all stood on the ramp of the ship
That would transport us to our new world
Somewhere out there amongst the stars
That had shed their light on our beloved planet Earth
For so many countless aeons.

Our beloved planet Earth, that had nurtured us
And protected us, fed us, kept us warm
Through so many countless generations
Now long since gone.

The long history of humanity is written down
In the scrolls that are our most treasured possessions
Apart from that of life itself.

But man had not respected what we should have held dear
And had torn our planet, our beloved Earth apart
With endless, futile wars, and the neutron bomb.

Man had misused his world, and abused it with pollution
Until the only solution was to leave his once-beautiful world
And leave it to complete its chosen path
Until it blew itself apart.

And so our ship left good mother Earth
And we stood on the observation deck
And saw our world slowly destroying itself
Until we saw the last vestiges of our once-mighty world
Becoming a glowing fireball in the realms of space.

And so we headed off to our new world
Even though this generation would never set foot
On what would be our new home.

And future generations would tell their children's children
That they were once, truly, children of the Earth.

John Marks

INVISIBLE THREADS

Invisible threads
Spun by spiders,
Criss-cross the trees,
Are turned in sun to silver,
Are everywhere,
Are strong as steel,
Are holding the wood together.

Invisible threads
Spun by lovers,
Weave in and out,
Are caught in glances,
And turned to gold,
Are strong as steel,
And gentle as a kiss,
Hold our lives
Together.

Margaret Black

A BASIC ART

I've learnt the art of writing.
Yes, sometimes I spell it rong.
The hardest part's expression,
mine doesn't sing a song.

I tried to pen a poem,
but struggled for a rhyme.
I couldn't bring the verse to life,
it happens every time.

I then wrote a short story,
but it hadn't got a plot.
A beginning and an ending,
that was about its lot.

Now I've bought a writing pad,
I'll practise and get better.
And if I stick to basics,
I might manage a letter.

Dawn Clayton

THE BEST THINGS IN LIFE ARE FREE

How much is a sunset worth?
Could you price a rainbow?
If you've heard the dawn chorus,
Its value would you know?

All these things are priceless,
When you talk of wealth,
Also in the list of values,
Near the top is health.

If we had to pay for these,
They'd be beyond our reach,
No-one has that kind of money,
They'd cost a fortune each!

Georgia B Jones

BABY SMALL

Looking, looking at the trees,
lying there so contented,
I wonder what he sees.
Sky so blue, bright breezy day,
makes the trees wild and sway.
Watching, seeing, movement and shapes.
Wide eyed wonderment written on his face.

What does he think of this big new world
It's hard to guess what he makes of it all,
When fed and full, has plenty to say
gurgling noises, sounds and faces pull,
little smiles of contentment and joy,
and then it's sleep for this little boy,
Oh, how I wish I was a baby small.

Janet A Hart

THE LIGHTHOUSE

In Withernsea town a lighthouse stands
It's not offshore it's just inland
Amidst the houses towering high
127 feet up into the sky
It was built in 1892
There's a museum inside, and a cafe too
144 steps for you to climb
Go up slowly, take your time
At the top, there's an open view
Of Withernsea and the coastline too.

Kathy Iley

WHAT'S HAPPENED TO GAINSBOROUGH

They tell me Gainsborough was a nice place two decades ago,
people were more friendly and let their inner-self show,
but those nice people have disappeared maybe out of time,
Now in the 1990's Gainsborough's a town of crime,
house burglaries have risen, more people are out of work,
there's drugs and vandalism, everywhere you turn,
what's happened, the town has such a bad name,
since those sunny days nothing's been the same,
now you daren't go out in case you are attacked in the street,
you don't know what to say, to anyone you meet,
what's happened to this town, a place I used to like?
Gainsborough has changed now, it's full of trouble and strife.

Claire Young

CONSTABLE COUNTRY

Do not think
of money:
Just freshness
broken colour
white speckled vistas
falling ground
acid yellow
and deep deep green.
Listen to the
sounds behind
times varnish.

Roy Sturgess

TO CELIA

Born in Peterboro', one of seven, that delicate babe
Our darling Mum and Nan, today has 80 made
Celia Mona has mellowed now, but you wouldn't have thought
She'd have reached this milestone after the illnesses she's caught
She, of course, had the usual ones that most kids get
But later on Diphtheria and Rheumatic Fever proved a very serious threat.
Still, she fought the germs and won, this lion-hearted lady
Although she was advised not to have a baby
Thank goodness her impulsiveness eventually shone through -
Giving life to John, David and later me, too!

Mum was a 'tinker' and daring in her youthful years
Sailing the North Sea in a rowing boat - with friends numbering three!
She would swim in the local river, near the old water mill
And I believe one admirer was a chap called Bill!
Perhaps he was a sax player in the popular dance band
In which our Mum was the vocalist - singing tunes of sentimental brand
The Co-op where she worked will probably never know
That she borrowed frocks to wear for the night - for her and sister Flo!
Anyway, Dad was naturally not deterred by this gal's behaviour
As their 59 year marriage proves - he obviously forgave her

She kept the home fires burning for him, when he went to war
With two little boys to care for - and fear for - life was never a bore
The terrors of those years could never be described
But we're all here today, 'cause our family survived
And so to this lady, who does everything with class
She's glamorous, charming, witty and has a certain pzazz!
On your special day, we give our best wishes and much love too
Because there are so few as precious to a family as you.

Denise Bennett

UNTITLED

Bells like a chiming,
Skirts need a lining
Birds like a nest,
or building feathers into a crest.
Boys like to joke,
The fire needs coke.
If you go out and the rain is pouring,
Look in the trees for the birds a snoring.

Joy Sharp

MY BAD DAY!

I got up this morning,
couldn't stop yawning,
I looked in the mirror, only to see . . .
the *real* me!
My hair was all over,
I looked like I had just been to Dover,
and back
with a rucksack,
My voice was all croaky,
the room was all smoky,
the wireless was blaring,
the sheep were marring,
the dog was barking,
the fire was sparking,
the chickens were chirping,
My sister was burping,
My toast was burning,
My stomach was churning,
So, I went to get dressed,
But didn't look my best,
the washer began to spin,
the sun went in,
Night time arrived,
so I dived
into bed
and said,
'Good night
sleep tight'

Sarah Kind (14)

OLIVE

Olive is strong and firm
Always wears a dress
Never blows her own trumpet
Is always there to help others
      out of a mess,
To provide tea and crumpets
With a cheerful face and voice.

P Boult

BEGGING I WOULD DO

Begging is not me
Crying too is not me
but if you walk away
I would beg you to stay
and crying my eyes out
because I would not want
to lose you so begging I would
do even crying to just
keep a hold of you.

C Rodrigues

WAS REALLY BEAUTIFUL

It was really beautiful
This view of the open countryside
That I wanted to stay forever
In leaving I could not just abide.

It was really beautiful
The air so nice and clean
Walking around so nice and free
On leaving I felt mean.

It was really beautiful
I come as often as I can
I wish I could buy a house near here
And live here all the time.

Keith L Powell

DIN'T NO 'ISS

din't no'iss yer

wa'er resis'an' mascara
recen'ly manicu'd nails
ring   woven   fingas
han' pain'id san' shoes
gold   ankal   bracele'
designa   sunglasiz
missin'   but'uns
snapped   shoe   lacez

on-ee no'issed you . . .

Barry P S Weldon

WHY?

Why, is house called house,
And bird called bird?
When you stop to think,
It's quite absurd!

I mean, why is word?

If it's fishes,
You have to say fish.
And if it's dishes,
You never say dish?

Or do you?

As in:
One sheep is called a sheep
But two of them
aren't sheeps.

Are they?

Do you spell it: T-H-E-I-R
or even T-H-E-R E?
And which witch is it
which?

All these rules I'd like to drop
Such as 'capital letters and a full stop'

But if word wasn't word
Then what on earth would it be?
And tell me why
Do the numbers start 0,1,2,3?

Alexa Sutton (12)

TO GARY FROM HIS NAN

We loved you, we miss you so very much.
No longer will we feel your touch
Or look upon your smiling face
As you after Denis chase
Or hear the car
At the end of the day
As you rush in asking
'What's for dinner eh?'
And when Christmas comes
There'll be an empty chair
A space beneath the tree
'Cause our Gary's not there
But we'll all meet again
In heaven up above
Together for ever
Wrapped in our Lord's love.

D Bacon

THE HEALER

When one you love is crying in pain
All you can do for them is done in vain,
You close your eyes and ask your God to spare
Them this ordeal - yet miracles are rare.
Yet see, the miracle is happening now.
For sleep the healer comes to show us how
Thro' sweet oblivion peace can be obtained
And health comes slowly back to be maintained.

Liz Hardgrave

DAWN IN WARD 4Y

A blackbird sings
The world stood still,
And as the silver notes
Began to spill
To my joy they flowed
To fill a hospital ward
And pain was stilled,
As though the stars
Had left the velvet night,
And come to dance
For our delight.

A Pullen

BEYOND THE SNOW

Christmas time is here again and the snow brings in icy chill
With all the festivities and decorations hails the season of goodwill
When children laugh and ride their sleighs across the whitened blanket
in time
And the families gather around the piano resounding in
Christmas rhyme

It's Christmas Eve and there's not much time left
To wrap those Christmas gifts
And the snow that's falling all around is making hills and rifts
Full to the brim with excitement and the kids wont go to bed
They say 'we're waiting for Santa
The big old man dressed in red'

It's Christmas Day and excitement rides high
And as you look out of the window snow is still falling from the sky
The children cannot open the presents quick enough
For there are still so many more, wrapping paper, cards and boxes litter
The once clean and tidy floor.

Around the table crackers are pulled and the noise floats from lip to lip
And of the sparkling wine both parents take an extraordinary large sip
Purely medicinal of course for it gets them through the day
It's only half past two and there's seven more hours to play

For the lonesome ones this Christmas seeking refuge from the night
Have the empathy of all men strive on and don't give up the fight
The atmosphere unquestionable it's Christmas time again
The snow that's falling all around will soothe away your pain.

But remember Christmas is not celebrated by everyone to many just
another day
They don't feel the warming presence of love or hear the Carols play
But let not their plight disturb you for they cannot miss what they do
not know
Although it does evoke questions and thought in your mind
As you find yourself looking *beyond the snow.*

Matthew Richardson-Harper

PASSING THOUGHTS

All that trash they used to write -
The swollen words of love-sick hearts -
Is now confined to mobile phones
And talk, talk, talk.

Love lies down in the outside lane -
A buzz of racing certainty -
And rambles there quite aimlessly
On, on and on.

Modern romance leaves no clues -
They're right to say it's good to talk -
The secret thoughts of high-speed love
Are lost, lost, lost.

Peter King

THROUGH CLOUDED EYES

My vision is so strange today, almost like a blur and I'm
too confused to ask the questions why,
All around is blackness in which nothing living stirs and
nothing that is wet seems dry.

My mind is playing tricks on me for usually I am warm, so
why am I shivering this way?
It usually gets this chilly just before a storm but I can see
the sun shine from where I lay.

There's something very wrong with me, I feel my heart
increase
but there's nothing I can do but watch the sky.
I'll swoop away from here when these feelings finally cease but
at the moment I'm much too weak to fly.

Another wave engulfs me as it slicks across the sand and
another carcass is washed up on the bay.
Why am I laying down when I really ought to stand? and why is
my breathing blocked this way?

It all seems very different to how it was before, before it
was all that I could wish.
It used to be so effortless to forage from the shore but it's
now become a contest for the fish.

From the south comes a silhouette and it lowers down a hand,
and it picks up the body of my mate.
Now it walks across to me but it fails to understand that
despite the help it's really much too late.

Is the world around me crumbling, are there species sadly
missed?
Are the silhouettes content to spread decay?
The lips of mother nature are somewhere needing to be kissed
and that need is growing stronger by the dayThere's a kind of peaceful
feeling settling in my mind and
it's unlike anything I've known.

If I should close my eyes then I think that I would find the
sky where the Phoenix once had flown.

Does he know I'm lifeless as he walks me up the beach?
Does he know that I'm no longer here?
Can he see me flying way out of his reach?
Once a again with feathers that are clear.

Ron Roberts

HEATWAVE

Another dawn
The sun is high
It shines so brightly
From the sky

I do a little,
Not a lot.
I'm just no good
When it's so hot

Give me good old English weather
Like we used to get
A bit of this, a bit of that
And rain that's cool and wet

Well, now we have that cool wet rain
It ne'er knows when to stop
So let me have some sun again
Then I'll complain (s'too hot)

Jean Perry

THE WALL

Do you ever think of me
behind that wall of yours?
Though time has passed
and life has changed my memories linger on.

You were my life, I worshipped you,
you'll never know how much I cared.
Life today is not the same
the day you left you took my soul.

I could have changed,
I would have changed, anything for you,
but the wall was built, high and strong.
Your love for me had gone.

A D Thomas

ENTERTAINING CHAPPIE

Arthur Askey Arthur Askey
What a guy,
He is just
So funny he
Makes me cry,
His funny jokes
and phrases make
me so happy,
He really was
a very entertaining chappie,
if he was around today
he would be the best,
but he is still a
legend so I'll leave
him to rest.

Tony Stocks

MY FRIEND AND I

My friend he stared at me through the glass door,
His big brown eyes quite big and round
His coat all askew.
My friend, he looked sorry while standing there,
'Please let me in,' he seemed to say.

We go for walks my friend and I.
The wheat is long and the grass is strong.
My friend he loves to weave in and out
Rushing to me with things that stick in his hair
We walked along, my friend and I
By the sluggish river
My friends tongue lolling out by then.

He looked into my eyes and then
towards the river
I picked up a stone, and threw as far as it would go
With a yell and a splash he jumped into that
sluggish river.
My friend he swam around, and to his delight,
he found my yellow stone.
I called to my friend,
He looked heavy and bedraggled
When he came to my side
My friend, he began to shake and shiver,
Sending droplets of rainbow water everywhere.
My friend, he licked my hand I stroked his head
Where we lay in the sun together
My faithful friend and I.

Wendy Nobbs

THE MOLECULE

Avrogadro said
All matter is composed of atoms
And atoms are indestructible and indivisible
If he spoke true it would have been
A peaceful world of shining suns
And silken scarves of interstellar hydrogen
But God, playing with his sticks and coloured beads
Like a precocious child with a gigantic Lego set
Invented the mighty molecule
Carbon, Hydrogen and Oxygen in endless chains
Which could reproduce themselves
By splitting down the middle
Like a zany zip fastener
Exactly as before
No not exactly
Sometimes there was a drop off
And mad Mendelic man was born
Who split the atom with a bang
That echoed round the universe
Did God really rest upon the seventh day
Or did he run away
Like the sorcerer's apprentice whose
Broom buckets threatened to flood the
Cosmic laboratory
If he did there will be
An almighty row
When the supreme Sorcerer returns.

E Carr

FANCY THAT

Plop! Tickety-plop!
Another alarm clock
thrown into the river.
Compact bronze helmeted
Horrors of technology
Carpeting the riverbed
Hundreds upon hundreds
of instant antiques.
Priceless at low tide
A marvel to behold
Some still tick,
Turn and time
in the humourless mud
that yearns to be sand
or even pebbles.

Robert Altass

LONELINESS

Loneliness is such a sad thing,
You know that people are there,
But you still feel in despair.
You still don't feel at peace,
Nor calm or at ease,
What can you do when you feel
        this way?
What can people say?
I guess you have to accept what
        you've got,
And that is yourself,
Always try to remember that you're
        worth a lot,
As hard as it may seem
You are special:
Don't let loneliness beat you.

Caroline Hill

HELP ME

I don't want to do this anymore
What is worth all this fighting for?
I just want to live in peace
Of all I deserve, that is the least.
Why can't people just let things go?
Am I safe or not? I never know
Always someone on my back
Claiming I've said this or that
I go about minding my own business
So why am I suffering like this?
The fear I have just can't go on
I've put up with it for so very long.
I'm sick with worry, always scared
But the pain inside cannot be shared.
I cry each night, always in vain,
I don't think I'll ever find freedom again.
I long to walk along the street
Without keeping my eyes towards my feet,
I want to hold my head up to the sky,
Without thinking, will I live or die?
It can't carry on, all over I'm sore
I've lost all vitality, don't like life any more.
Someone please protect me from hatred dealt,
I'm not strong enough to fight back for myself,
I'm too weak, can't shield the hurt,
Stop the blows and kicks, keep me out of the dirt.
I want to smile for real, don't want to taste the tears,
Please, someone, anyone, wash away my fears.

Lisa Lovelock

AUTUMN JEWELS

As through the woods I gaze and see,
Autumn unfolding its magic all around me.
Leaves, in silence, descend upon my head,
Carpeting the ground to soften my tread.

A squirrel gathering its winter store,
Scurries off, then back for more.
Raindrops, that fall upon the trees, now seep,
Their branches, in jewelled perfection, weep.

Soon they will be standing bare,
Exposed to the winter's chilling air.
Rays of the sun, when the rain gives way
Brilliant orange, take the last glimpse of day.

A harvest mouse slips silently by,
A wary fox, so sleek, so sly,
A badger sniffs the evening air,
Wood pigeons cooing, haven't a care.

Soon the moonlight, casting its light so pale,
Will cover everything with its silver veil;
And through the silence of the night,
Around me, autumn's magic; sheer delight!

Jeff Saundercock

EARLY BIRD

How bright the blackbird's beady eye
His beak how sharp and keen.
And yellow as a celandine
In sunny spring or summertime.
He hops and stares,
Then stops and glares,
No lowly quarry seen.

With coal-black feathers ruffled up
In early light a-glistening.
Now still, he stands and stares, then stamps,
To left and right a-listening.

But blind to blackbirds' eager beaks,
The unsuspecting worm,
As 'twixt the emerald blades it glides.
With yellow flash and final squirm
Down feathered throat it slides.

Roger Rayment

WHERE WILD FLOWERS GROW

In some lovely untrodden place
  where wild flowers grow,
I leave my distant memories
  with my youth of long ago.

Together with the sunshine
  of warm and happy years
I leave my apprehension
  and forget the times of tears.

I remember most the best things
  when music filled my heart,
When youngness seemed eternal,
  and life, I was a part.

But because I sense the twilight
  through the calm of closing days,
I now look back along my path
  in judgement of my ways.

And all in all, if I can judge,
  though saint I'll never be,
My soul unfettered will repose
  where souls abide quite free.

So when I die, just one request;
  please spread my ashes low,
In some lovely untrodden place
  where wild flowers grow.

Keith Hutchins

WIVES

Wandering through the crowds of the boulevard,
She spots the shop she needs.
Bursting through the door,
She escapes from the beggars and the buskers.

As she browses she hears the sound,
Of the monotonous beat,
Of new age music.

Spotting a friend, she moves towards her,
Over the sound of the shop,
The till beeping and alarms sounding at the door.
They begin to chat about the builder down the road,
And the clothes in the shop.

Pressed for time the two friends part.
Taking the clothes she likes,
Regardless of the price,
She pays for them with your money.

Leaving the shop,
She continues down the boulevard,
Past the tempting smells of jacket potatoes and hot dogs.

Reaching the multi-storey car park,
She meets you.

Matthew Afford (12)

HOW PRECIOUS

Setting sun, stars that glow,
clouds that form, rain and snow.
Watching everything grow.
How precious is sight.

Children's laughter could be heard,
the sound of rippling waves, birds.
Noises now that once were words.
How precious is sound.

Beautiful, fragrant flowers,
scent of herbs that lasts for hours.
Smelling grass after showers.
How precious is smell.

Like leaves our bodies flutter down,
eventually beneath the ground.
Life still goes on all around.
How precious is life.

M E Pack

SOOTY

We've a beautiful cat, named *Sooty,*
He's *black,* from his head to his toes,
But next door, our neighbour's *a gardener,*
And he and Sooty, *are foes.*

One day, at a garden centre,
He bought a bird bath, and a stand,
But when he forgot to *add water,*
Things didn't go as he'd planned.

When Sooty was prowling his garden,
Into that bird bath, he peeped,
He climbed in, and made himself comfy,
And thought, what a nice place to sleep.

Every day, when Sooty got tired,
In that bird bath, he'd take his nap,
When our neighbour looked out of his window,
He didn't see birds . . . *just our cat.*

Then, early the very next morning,
When Sooty jumped up, for his nap,
That bird bath had been filled with water,
And Sooty, *was one surprised cat.*

He hovered above that bird bath,
He just wasn't sure what to do,
Then to his surprise, *and amazement,*
He pulled up his feet, *and he flew.*

Since then, when our neighbour sees Sooty,
His face breaks into a grin,
And, even though they *aren't friendly,*
He has a soft spot, for him.

Pauline Markham

A FAVOURITE WALK

From Norman church to Norman bridge and back again.
Who, down through the ages, have enjoyed that walk?
Do ghosts from the past glide through meadow and parkland,
along the riverside, where once they used to stroll and talk?

And, if they do, what then of more recent spirits,
of those who, remembered still, are loved and mourned?
Do they, too, take that pleasant, well-trodden path
that once they walked and with their presence adorned?

And what of you, my love, my sweetheart and best friend?
Does your spirit keep pace beside me still, and pause and rest,
as, not so very long ago, you did yourself,
along that old familiar trail you loved the best?

James Dalgleish

PEACE

A peace within the spirit
is a place without turmoil,
hate and confusion,
a soul that travels anywhere
without conflict.
It's a freedom that doesn't
require food to eat,
air to breathe,
water to drink,
or sun to shine -
but radiates within, without
and forever.

Jan H Hitchcock

TO THE CHILDREN OF DUNBLANE

The children of Dunblane
will in our hearts remain
their lives had just begun
when that awful man with the gun
shot them down

We all have to feel
for their families, friends and chums
they've had to bear the grief
and silent fear

So get rid of all the guns
Parliament if you please
then children can have fun
and live no more in fear of the guns.

Sandra McKinnon

MANMADE DESPAIR

I see their eyes,
Shining so dull,
I hear their cries,
Which arms will not cull.

I smell their neglect,
left to wallow and rot,
Hidden away to forget,
In a sad, lonely cot.

I remember their stare
So pleading and selfish,
To have love which to share,
Is their one dying wish.

We don't see them existing,
Just an image in our head,
But their plight is inflicting,
They're unloved, they're unfed.

I hear them calling,
For anyone to come,
My tear drops start falling,
As nothing is done.

I feel despair,
As I watch in a trance,
So much to repair,
Someone give them a chance.

Caroline Rowan

UNTIL DEATH US DO PART
(?)

I was there
Said the fly
On ceiling high.
Alone then he died
Asked I?
Not so, replied
The fly.

At last drawn breath
Death's shadow dark
Was flung aside
And just as mist
Flees from the sun
A presence warm
Stood by his side.

In health we shared
Much happiness,
The vision said.
And then distress
When sickness struck
Confining me to chair
Then bed.
So much you cared
And did your best,
Until the shadow came
To relieve me of the pain
And give you rest.

But now this angel 'Death'
In turn unites again
Two lonely hearts.
Together go, said he
And stand you strong.
Then, with one accord
Affirm again
Your Christian vows,
This time, before the Lord.

Ken Knell

A BORING SUNDAY RECIPE

Take several oversize people
Squeeze into too small Sunday suits
Sprinkle on a few hats and walking sticks
Add two pinches of wedding, weather and
                                    family talk.
Push into cold wooden pews and mix in one
                          hour long sermon.
Put in rows and drag out into hot sunshine
Roast for one hour in a small kitchen.
Slowly mix in a few vegetables and potatoes.
Put in one big armchair and leave for two hours.
Then polish up and decorate.
Sprinkle on a bit of Songs of Praise.
Cut up and eat.
Put the rest in one big quilt and leave until mouldy.

Michelle Afford (14)

CHANGE OF STATUS

Scruffy scrap of paper
Never had a place,
Stuck inside a catalogue
In the writing case.

For years and years it stayed there
Tattered and forlorn.
Then one day I had a thought -
The time was early dawn.

I felt the urge to write
A poem there and then;
My writing pad was missing -
I only had my pen.

Then that little scrap of paper
Fluttered into view,
So I sat and wrote my poem
My darling, just for you!

C Francis

A XMAS-TIME CAROL

Xmas time is here once again - its story to tell
As I hear, in the distance, the singing of the 'First Noel'

The snow glistens brightly in the moonlight,
As their footprints are left behind
peace on Earth to all mankind

Xmas time is special for all children - early
to bed on Xmas Eve
To dream of all those presents from Santa
They have been patiently waiting to receive

The carol singers are now homeward bound,
Their entertainment done
They too look forward to festive food and fun

Peace in our time over all the world
may it one day, come true
A very merry Xmas and happy New Year,
To each and every one of you.

J M Greenacre

CHARLIE'S HUTCH

A rabbit hutch I'm going to make,
Don't know how long it's going to take.
I gather some bits of wood together,
At least it is fine sunny weather.

I size the wood with my tape measure.
This will be a hutch my child will treasure.
I saw each plank to the right length,
And all of a sudden I run out of strength.

I have a biscuit and a cup of tea,
Now I feel better, more like me.
I fetch the hammer and the nails,
I am careful not to walk on the snails.

Each piece of wood I nail in place,
Taking my time as it is not a race.
With weather proofing and a mesh door,
Charlie the rabbit could ask for no more.

Sheila Hutchinson

BSE

BSE
What does it mean to you and to me?
Farmers in rage, cattle slaughtering,
Confidence down, the economy faltering.
Politicians in conflict, public hysteria,
Details abound in all of the media.
Illness and suffering, through CJD,
That's BSE in you and me.
Nervous systems in disarray,
How many cases will appear today?

Paul William Hutchinson

UNTITLED

O what have we done to
this earth that was given to us
on the little time we are on it

Since man has come on the earth
He has brought with him disruption
And destruction he is like a stranger
In the night he takes from the earth
And leaves it like a desert

And what of the animals birds and fish
Man thinks this world belongs to him alone
but it does not God has given man power
over animals so look after them don't kill them
Give them freedom and space

For what is man without beast
For what happens to beast soon
will happen to man

Continue to contaminate your earth
And you will one day suffocate
In your own waste.

M W Lowe

WORLD

World so wonderful,
Full of light,
All around beauty,
Of day and night.
The silent innocence,
Of cats that roam,
Looking to find,
Their familiar path home.
A harvesting squirrel,
Perched on a fence,
Nibbling a nut,
Silently tense.
Birds gather,
Waiting for the worm,
Bigger birds diving,
For their turn.
Children playing,
In the autumn leaves,
With laughter in their hearts,
And dirt on their knees.
Beauty in the world,
Will always shine through,
The beauty you can see,
And the beauty you do.
World so wonderful,
Full of light,
All around beauty,
Of day and night.

Jessica Macdonald

RADIANCE

When the green dragon of the east,
is followed by the white tiger of the west,
The icy mansion heralds strange encounters,
Southern summers fire bird is just a jest.

Monarch of the purple palace,
Respect the rule of the Great Bear.
Wood planet Jupiter is in the Temple,
Metal Venus influence can be so rare.

No tortoise palace, no black, no winter.
Water and north, you must be there.
Not so, say the notional mansion.
Its imagination, human life is not fair.

Heaven's reward, a strong yin,
Finds itself totally at home.
The Red Phoenix, fortunate but yang,
is isolated, so very all alone,

Your soul is in Heaven's emptiness,
An unfortunate star, and very yin.
So true self under the microscope,
Believe in yourself. You can win.

B L Haswell

MY LOCAL

Place of activity, gossip and chat
a nice atmosphere as I step on the mat.
Each day someone different: is serving and helping,
with customers delving through bargains on shelving.

On Mondays it's quiet and not very busy,
the lady who helps then, I think is called Lizzie
more ladies upstairs, sort, iron, and label
they have quite a laugh, when they're working with Mabel!

There's clothes for all seasons, sizes and shapes,
modern day fashions to old-fashioned capes.
For children and babies, ladies and gents
sometimes a great bargain, for just a few pence!

There's bric-a-brac: books, and items for cooks,
hats, handbags, and even a thing there with hooks!
some items are mysteries what are they for?
yet, somebody buys them and comes back for more!

With regulars weekly, it's more like a club
of what do I write, church hall, or the pub?
Oh no! It's the 'charity shop' just down the street,
who support needy children, in 'finding their feet!'

Beryl Lenihan

THE LEGACY

When I'm old as old can be
And in a rest home by the sea
And people come and say to me
'Have we drunk our cup of tea?'
I shall say in words so clear
'I don't know if *we* have, my dear
But I have not - can't stand the stuff
Just pass the snuff, and where's me fags and beer?'

And I'll remind them every day
of all the thousands stashed away
And intimate that, if they're kind,
I will likely have a mind
To leave them something in my Will
Just for a rainy day

And they will try so hard to please
They'll bring a blanket for my knees
And beer and fags they'll smuggle in
And hopefully, a little gin!
And when I'm gone, with faces sad
They'll say 'The best we've ever had'
And gather round to hear the Will
With eyes aglow and voices still
And then, so dazed and woebegone
As lawyer says in awful tone
She's left it to the cats' home!'

Carol A Dickens

LISTEN NOT BEAUTY

I am not very well read
and I read not very well
but the thoughts that harbour in my head
I wish for you to tell

Listen not beauty or tranquil peace
for I'm not sure that you will approve
of the words that are of the very least
uncertain and written too crude

I interpret as I see
and will to the end not know in heart
if I have or will succeed
to please to the finish and from the start.

Daniel T O'Neill

SHATTERED DREAM

One day I thought of moving
To this old house by the sea
Full of joy and excitement
I called to collect the key,
From outside the house was inviting
With all roses round the door
The garden had grown up to waste
And the outlook was very poor
Anyway I turned the key
I thought I'd have a peep
Inside the room hung cobwebs
And the stairs were very steep
By now I was feeling shaky
This house had something to say
Should I stay and listen
Or shall I turn and go away
Just when I thought I'd seen enough
Something touched my head
I stood and froze and shook with fright
Have I met up with the dead
I never even turned around
Just made it straight to the door
My dreams were quickly shattered
Of living in that house by the shore.

Dinah Holt

MEANING TO LIFE

There must be a meaning to our life
  each path must have a reason
The same as leaves upon a tree
  they change and fall each season
But like the trees some are strong
  while others must fight forever
Some people must battle all their life
  yet others will battle never
But who decides which path we go
  and who decides what reason
Like who told trees they had to follow
  each and every season
I pray now for the spring to come
  when the damp dead leaves are gone
For spring is green and fresh to smell
  and everything is growing strong.

Lisa Bristow

POPPY DAY

Lines run deep across his brow,
Rheumy eyes clouded, as remembrance told me how,
deep, so deep, the memories lay, tight within him,
Seeping out, on days such as now.
Though bent with age, he had once stood proud,
Snapped to attention at the sergeant's growl.
His lips lifted, a remembered smile, of long dead friends,
Who march with him now, voices, one by one replay in
his mind, though long silenced by shell and gun.
Horrors understood by those who were there,
Cause a tear to run down a path well marked and used to them.
As hoarse his voice quivers to speak,
'Alfred, my mate, Bill and Charlie Leech.'
Defensively, his voice is raised,
'We were proud to go,'
'It were our duty - you know,'
'Though that seems strange, these days.'
No, no, I shook my head,
Thinking of my young son's school, determined to remember
the debt,
With two minutes silence, all that we owe,
Young men who died, to children now, so long ago.
With blood red poppies, we will teach,
They too will remember, Alfred, Bill and Charlie Leech.

Sheila Lowrie

FUTURE THOUGHTS

It's hard to feel bright about the future, when the future seems so bleak
The news around us sounds so sad, we feel outrage every week
Is there a future for my generation, or more importantly, the next?
Should this be a thing to just hope for, or something we should expect?
We shouldn't have to survive on hope alone, something needs to be done
I can't see things changing overnight, the battle has only just begun
How do we make things better when the situation has got so bad?
Somehow, we have to make it different, to obtain what we once had.

Sheryl Roach

ODE TO OLD FELIXSTOWE

The house on the cliff was grandpa's,
He's long since gone sadly,
It's where I spent my childhood,
As a lad here by the sea.

Still limpets cling to the rugged rocks,
The seagulls hover above in flocks,
Rippling waves surround our dock,
As all my memories now unlock.

Seashells and sand adorn the bay,
The lighthouse flashes the night away,
The beach huts help to shade our day,
As this telescopic view portrays.

Cockles, mussels, crab meat too,
The fishermen catch it all for you,
Their little boats go out at night,
When old Felixstowe is a warm delight.

Lobster pots were boiling,
In our cottage by the sea,
Where horseshoes enhanced the doorway,
Now it all belongs to me.

Oh how I miss you grandpa,
And the days sat on your knee,
But it's my turn to play the part you played,
In our expanding family tree.

Your rocking chair in the watch tower,
Looks over the headland and far,
As my little grandson rushes up to me,
And asks for stories from the past.

Diana Dooner

WHO CARES FOR THE CHILDREN

Children, welcome to an adult world,
who gives you warning?
Who helps you in your fight against fate?
More pain in the world than you'll ever guess
and yet you blunder forth unguided,
why don't we warn our children -
        against love?

It will break their hearts and may
devour their souls.
Shouldn't our children be taught on the important things,
        when adults are a-fool in love
        what chance have children?

Fate can be guided if warned against
if experience were to be taught as well as gained
we could learn thricethold
and our children would reap the harvest we sow.
So why don't children go into the world pre-armed,
lust warned against, the traps of vice
known, so at least when their sprung
they would be so knowingly?
If knowledge is a sin, what of ignorance?

Cliff Homewood

THE MEANING OF MUSIC

Messages in music may not at first be clear,
But they can be uncovered after each piece you hear.
Singers show their feelings, and their thoughts
                              they do share,
Hoping understanding people are listening out there.

Music is not just words which some person chants,
And which others sing along to when they want a
                              cheerful dance.
Music can teach you lessons to make you think hard,
Like the touching words in a pretty greetings card.

Elaine Ede

DUNBLANE - NEVER AGAIN

We all know of the tragedy that took place at Dunblane
But why did it have to happen - it was absolutely insane
So many young lives just wasted and brought to an end
For what? we all ask, but cannot comprehend.

It seems society today goes from bad to worse,
Too much freedom and temptations are an absolute curse
It is time that the country woke up to reality
And did something positive to prevent such a calamity.

The main question here is what do we do about guns?
The government must react to criticisms from which the
answer comes
And the only real solution has been made abundantly clear
Is to ban all forms of firearms, which most people fear.

To the fanatics who practice shooting and say it's a sport
I say - it's a dangerous past- time that should never be taught.
Whilst the owners of guns may well guard their possessions
These objections of death do sometimes reach hands
with obsessions.

It is, therefore, most important that early action is taken
Before we have yet another disaster, and life is forsaken.
So, my plea to the government is quite simple and plain
Please, let's not have another tragedy, just like Dunblane.

Edwin J Hughes

MURPHY'S LAW

Murphy was around at breakfast time,
                    invoking his law.
I could tell by my buttery toast
                    stuck to the floor.

I shouted at him, 'Come out, you coward!
                    and show yourself,'
Waving a letter from the taxman
                    reducing my wealth.

The car got a flat and the dog fleas,
                    all before lunch.
Supper? I was ready for the power cut
                    - just had a hunch.

Exhausted, I fell into my unmade bed.
                    'Please, no more to follow!'
But Murphy gave a departing chuckle,
                    Friday 13th tomorrow!

C Barker

FORBIDDEN LOVE

Can we go on feeling like we do
When on *his* day, he said *'I do'*
We thought it was to last
The love we have, is it really in the past
The lies, the hurt, we have both been through
We can carry on, if we are both true
We both know it is wrong to feel
But can't seem to stop or to heal
One day, we will realise our true fate
I hope it never turns to hate
What in the meantime do we do
Simply to say - 'I love you.'

J Money

CHANGES

Oceans return as rain
Everything comes back again
Time changes what we see
But life is as it has to be
Materials we throw away
Come to life another day
Laughing sparkling eyes
Turn to dark screaming cries
The energy man fails to understand
Yelling us this Earth is
Our precious living hand.

W E Mead

ANGLIAN WONDERLAND

East Anglia in dawn's morning, heralds a chorus of birdsong low and high,
Broadlands reflecting sunlight, the trilling song of skylarks echoes
in your sky,
A panorama of dormant beauty, creates a pristine vision upon
virgin ground,
Creatures of the wildwoods bathe in your sunlight, in a mystical
peace newly found.

East Anglia in evening's sunset, skies painted red and pink all aglow,
Silhouetting circling wildfowl, as soaring in thermals they steadily
climb and go,
Across fens an orchestra of reed beds, whispers sweet music
to our ears,
Gentle breezes kiss still waters, expanding ripples catch our tears.

East Anglia in early springtime, creating new landscapes of
red and blue,
Wooded glades carpeted by bluebells, adding splendour to our view,
Dogrose and violet decorate woodland rides, a fritillary butterfly
glides by,
A resonant drumming of a spotted woodpecker, echoes from trees
and fills the sky.

East Anglia in warm mid-summer, weasels and red fox prowl and run,
Nature alive in peaceful harmony, bursting with energy until
the day is done,
A natural order of flora and fauna, stretches as far as our eyes can see,
No wanton killing or destruction, just tranquillity for you and for me.

East Anglia in late autumn, golden leaves fall thick and still,
A kaleidoscope of changing colours, gives a new identity
to nature's will,
New hues and shades in great wildwoods, heralds in a different day,
Like the autumn of our own lives, holds a different meaning
along the way.

East Anglia in mid-winter, a white landscape, giant firs stand as
                                                    sentinels on guard,
Copious flood waters are still now, frozen ice, and the land bone hard,
Some creatures chose to hibernate, ferns of frosty filigree
                                                    pattern ground,
A curlew's lonesome cries, mingle with hungry seagulls, in a
                                                    harmony of sound.

East Anglia you colour four seasons, giving an eastern promise
                                                    of delights,
Heralding in a natural order, constantly thrilling us with new sights,
We sense from within this order, a magical hidden hand
                                                    is reaching out,
And feast our eyes with new wonders, painting fresh pictures
                                                    all about.

Jim Wilson

REFLECTIONS

I am
A corner, deprived of light
An endless alley-way in an endless night
A deserted pub with no ale to booze
A drowsy parent who yearns for a snooze

I am
Death who's lost its scythe
Buried in a coffin but still alive
A distressed dog encaged in a car
A traveller's weary feet which have plodded too far

I am
The punishment that everybody fears
A yelling, felled tree that nobody hears
Can you hear shouting from deep within?
No-one will know me beneath the skin.

Michael Sumsion

LILLIPUTIAN FAIRYLAND

Summer's evening a warm whispering
Kiss of breeze upon my cheek
I walk through damp grass
And smell honeysuckle's' heady scent
The whirring wings of hawk moths
Attending each flower like
Airborne waiters in flight
And then before me I behold
A village in miniature of tiny lights
Like Gulliver I feel
As I look down upon them.
Gleaming jewels of mint green.
The glow worm's beacon of love
To its suitor up above
They meet and pair with saddened air
And then dimming theatre lamps
They part and die but not in vain
The eternal return will see a
New beginning of terrestrial stars
To catch the eye.

Michael Joseph Lafferty

KARAOKE QUEEN

She sang her heart out the other night,
But she did not win.

She brought the house down the other night,
But she did not win.

She danced and gyrated, her body language stated that she was in
control of the song,
But seventh heaven would soon be flat, for her anticipation was wrong.

When female pride is shattered,
Hell's fury will break loose.
Venom splattered everywhere,
The judge must face the noose.

Stephen Friede

WAIT AND SEE

Thanks for always being there:
For showing just how much you care.
For being a lover and a friend,
knowing our friendship will never end.
Our time together goes so fast,
I wish for longer, it would last.

Feel warm and safe, when I'm with you.
Worries, well I've had a few:
Ghosts from the past, that won't lie down;
sometimes haunt me and make me frown.
But that was He, and you are You;
hard to let go and start something new.

Might go back, if he wanted me:
Perhaps I should set you free?
No way can I make a choice.
You know the truth: You have the voice;
To want me round, the way I am.
I care for you, That's no 'sham'.

I see you nearly every day:
Would miss you so much, if you went away.
I only hope that you will stay,
but that is not for me to say!
Time will show us what is right.
We may be together, for all our 'goodnights'.

I miss you now, when we're apart.
That is definitely a start!
I care for you, there is no doubt:
Just let time work it out.
Today we're together, you and me;
As for tomorrow: let's wait and see.

Martina Peters

50 GOLDEN YEARS

They first met in the Air Force
Len thought she was a peach
It was down in Cambridgeshire
In the camp at Waterbeach.

They had their first kiss whilst at this camp,
Underneath the mistletoe,
At the Christmas celebrations there,
Back in forty three you know.

They wed in nineteen forty six,
Our Len was full of pride,
With Ruby at the altar,
When she became his bride.

Yes, over the years, as we all do,
They've had their ups and downs,
But finished up triumphant,
With many more smiles than frowns.

Moving now to their twilight years,
If they could recast their nets,
They would take those self same vows again,
As they have no regrets.

So now to Len and Ruby,
And I say this most sincere,
We all wish you the best of health,
And the very best of cheer.

Now enjoy your anniversary,
On this twelve of October,
I think we can forgive you both,
If you're not entirely sober.

Peter J Sutton

THE WAITING ROOM

An axe of lead
Destroys the soul
A sweeping black cloud
Of increasing frustration
Tearing up neurones
And ripping up feelings
Playing with intellect
And stripping emotions
Smoke all those cigarettes
Ease all that tension
Blank, lead and dulling
Pent-up. Cessation.
Smash up vitality
Crack brick against bone
Drink all that caffeine
Leave those matches to burn
Dissolve interest in stupor
Reach that stale and drugged state
Numbed by those dregs
Being forced to stagnate.

Clare Phillips

NEWHAM IN ESSEX

We go to Kent to go hopping,
There is no stopping down hopping
We come back home in lorries
Because we are Cockneys
We sing 'With an ee I ho ee
I o, hee I ee I o,'
Our own hopping song.
We pick hops in September.
We do not forget to remember our home
In East Ham, Custom House Silvertown,
Plaistow and Canning Town in *Essex*
We visit our friends in Little Bardfield in *Essex,*
Who were evacuated from the docks in
Custom House, East London in *Essex*
We were bombed badly and scattered over
The country from Wales to Wiltshire beneath the
White Horse of Edington.
We all wished to return to our bombed out home in
Custom House, Canning Town in East London in *Essex.*
We go to Southend on Sand from Newham.
We combine all these districts together to make
one big area called Newham
                In *Essex!*

Rose Nicholson

LOST LOVE

It's great you and I
I know we will survive
The pain and hurt of loving you.

Make your wrongs right
stand by you through our plights
In return I'll only learn
You'll hurt me.

You know you hold my heart
So why are we apart
Our ups and downs we've lived them through
You know I'm meant for you.

I'll wait for your return
I know I'll never learn
To hide this pride because deep inside
This love's so strong
It can't be wrong.

It's great you and I
I know we will survive
It's great you and I
I know we will survive . . .

Isabelle Wright

MY BED

My bed!
So snug and warm.
My bed!
Get up in the morning on a cold
day brings chills to my spine
having to get out of . . .
My bed!
In the bath get dressed go to
school (6 hours later) home
Watch TV then in my jarmies
and off to . . .
My bed!

Emma Wilding (10)

SECRET LOVE

Sweet secret love in fleeting moments spent
Discreet the flattering smile on tempting lips
The joy of meeting occasionally by chance
Friendship that absence only can enhance

Shy secret love with winged emotions full
Jaded male on physical attractions satisfied
Ego sustained by gesture and imagination
New love that walks with shadows everywhere.

Nomadic instincts lead to quiet country lane
Isolated thoughts rush through the troubled mind
Forever in the heart sad keen desire
Eager to possess love that's out of reach

Recurring like the breeze the sacred marriage vows
Principles on which real love is built.
Stolen love that invents cruel little white lies
Creating in the mind embarrassed guilt

Enchanted thoughts no sorrow in pure minds
But conscience unaware of physical desire
Secret love demure with character and charm
Wanting love yet ever fearful and alarmed

A kiss and cuddle hot exploring hands
Searching for love purists do not understand
Throbbing flesh erect alone of conscience born
Unaware of bitterness or situation so forlorn

Come secret love enjoy the ecstasy now
Let mind and body drift in perfect unison
Hot breath and burning kisses everywhere
Love spent exhausted limp moistened hair

Amorous advances heaping coals upon the fire
Mind wrapped in torture bodies with desire
Secret love fulfil my yearning thoughts
And body with sweet stolen secret love.

William A Harding

ANIMAL COUNTRY

Animal country is falling down
The lion roars
And flees his crown
The hyena laughs
No more or dares
For hills of green
Are concrete stairs
The monkey on a one-way track
Goes tree to tree
With no way back
Then the noise
Of a moving man
Who thinks he has the extensive plan
I have all your land he says
Then came a sound of a saw,

> Roar
> You have, you have
> also our law.

Edward Lee Crosby

EAST ANGLIAN SPRING

In the yawning dawning of the chill April morning,
In the springing singing of birds gaily winging,
And the roiling boiling of surf ever toiling
On the sand and the shingle that skirts our east shore.

In the thriving writhing of spray ever rising,
And calling and bawling at each rise and falling
Of tides, swelling and welling and thunder clouds belling
On the sand and the shingle that skirts our east shore.

In the caging raging of the spring tides rampaging,
In the lengthening strengthening pale sun's adventuring,
Spring is racing, chasing, forever embracing
The sand and the shingle that skirts our east shore.

C D Isherwood

OUR MUMS

Mothers are so special
There's a bond so very strong,
They give you love and understanding
And to them we do no wrong,
When it comes the time to lose them
Our hearts are filled with sorrow,
And we know a loved one's gone
For today and all tomorrows.
But love and memories will
               always be there
Until our very end
For she was not only our mother
But also our best friend.

Valerie Gates

WORKING GIRL

She lay sun hot against the noon day rock.
Unfettered toes she flexed in cool damp sand.
With skin still goosed from promised truant swim
Her mind was torn between herself and work.
From one till two her lunch-time break, he'd said;
Now ten to three, how could she stay? But still
Her body yearned to lay on warming rock.
Another half an hour her senses craved
And yet she knew the risk could cost her job.
Smith, Carter, Dobbs solicitors at law,
It said upon the name-board on the stair
And Harold Carter pushed his glasses high
'Where is that girl?' Annoyance showing through
But underneath annoyance there was more -
A hopeless thrill, impossible to stem.
Her breathy, elfin presence made him weak
And steamy thoughts confused his afternoon.
And when at last she stood before him, meek,
His fruitless show of anger disappeared.
She knew, she knew deep down she'd won the day
But guilt dissolved the pleasures of the skin.

D M Beale

THE EXPERIENCE OF TIME

How do we get through life?
By going on and finding new ways to feel
time is passing, has significance
and meaning, by sticking to old ways
refusing every time to remember
how they have all been stuck to before, feigning
surprise at the familiar conclusions
saying we have learned what already we knew.

How do we keep on going?
By climbing each mountain, crossing each bridge, speaking
Of progress, evolution and development, then
avoid that chance glanced face in the mirror
that reminds you how starkly you are unchanged
a child still, only the surface is different,
hardened and settled, become more defined
in the time it has taken to write these few lines.

Howard Young

MISSED A RIGHT?

Are you bored of going out with blokes who know your mates
They think it's fun to set you up with gay or balding dates
You've gone out to a night-club and some bloke asks you out
But you turn around and there he is, another lager lout
It's dismal being single, I fear the future's black
But worse if you're unlucky enough to date an anorak!
Fed up with feeling awful, watching movies all alone
I forced myself to meet someone, I went out on my own
I'm sitting in this singles bar, Martini on the rocks
Enclosed by wimps and funny limps and blokes in party frocks!
'Fancy a drink?' a deep voice said, Mr Right could it be he?
He was smart and polite but I thought all night,
                that his dress would look better on me!
But when it hits the weekend, it's just me, the girls and the Stellas
Until at the end when there's only me 'cos they've all run off with fellas
So here I am the following night, playing the gooseberry
But no longer looking for Mr Right 'cos he can come and find me.

Surria Khan

MERRY-GO-ROUND

Life is a very, always a very, merry-go-round
keeping you guessing, keeping you guessing, that's what I've found
Round every corner, at every step, surprises abound
While this old world keeps on turning.

We have to take both the good and the bad
That's how it always will be
Sometimes be happy and sometimes be sad
That's only fair you'll agree

Time after time you climb up and then you fall down
Time after time you're clever and then you're a clown
Time after time you're smiling and then comes a frown
But all the time we keep learning.

We have to take both the good and the bad
That's how it always will be
Sometimes be happy and sometimes be sad
That's only fair you'll agree.

Geoff O'Neil

MY DAUGHTER

Oh my woeful, unpredictable, lovely daughter
Why do you torment me so?
Oh my beautiful, wonderful, horrid child
Why do you want to leave me and go?

You're the child in the middle
That may not be fair
But I couldn't predict
Which one would be there

One day you are up
The next you are down
Sometimes so serious
With always a frown

You put such a brave face
On all that you do
You feel that the whole human race
Is against you

The chip on your shoulder
Becomes a steep hill
When I pull rank
And say 'Yes you will!'

If only you'd let me into your sphere
You'd find me a friend, so close and so dear
If only you'd let me into your thoughts
I'd be able to help when you're feeling so wrought.

Carol Templey

ONCE

Alone and forgotten on the window sill
This weary lovelock stands
Withered and dry, faded by sun
It may look lost now, but it has seen some fun.

This wonderful plant simply grown from a seedling
Nurtured with trust, respect and care
It flourished with each and every new feeling
As two hearts combined and made a pair.

Growing as one from the roots to the tips
Each perfect petal a brush of the lips
Full of colour, joy and energy
Swaying in the breeze happy and free.

Now this love has sorely gone
Only the structure remains
Memory of a love gone long
No sign of the life it once contained.

Now the seasons have turned
These two hearts both have learned
That despite the heartache and times they've wept
This is a memory that will always be kept.

Katie Williams

BOYHOOD DREAMS

Was it true that long ago
winters always came with snow,
and did I dream when I was young
that tender earth and harvest sun
among the flaxen meads of hay
were always with me, every day.
Was awareness more intense
when up and over wicket fence
I'd run across the endless fields
where bold adventures were so real
where greenwood trees were wide and high
for me to climb, to touch the sky.
Everywhere a place to hide, every colour magnified.
Scrumping in the orchard bed
fearful of the farmer's tread,
clear cool springs, to dip my feet
to drink the crystal water sweet,
bonds and trysts, and solemn vow
made to keep, forgotten now
lost in time through clogging mist
never knew how we were kissed,
by the early dew of life
long before the cares and strife
changed the way we hear and see,
leaving fragile memory.
O please may I, before life dies
see again, through boyhood eyes.

Bob Putt

GOODBYE HOMO SAPIEN

Erected pylons protruding high
Ugly skyscrapers collected by
Stagnated ponds overrun with filth and trash
Why is modern man so rash.

With waste and sewage he doesn't care
Contaminates land and poisons air
Destroying wildlife species rare
For killing has a natural flair.

The seas he's killed he'll find in time
It's oil and effluent not salt and brine
But still he doesn't mind
Is it too late for mankind.

Just think what the tide will bring, with
Its foam
The beach will be no place to roam
No more the world we know and love
The rain of nuclear dust from above
Will mutate children not yet born
Blind maim and deform

So you see everyone must act
Doomsday is near and that's a fact
The odour of decomposing filth will bring
A day of death to the Homo Sapien
The rotting world will die of shame
With only itself to blame.

No-one can say we were not told
Man himself has cast the mould
So stop pollution and surmising
Only then shall we see a new dawn arising.

Try to think of the world we know
The wind the sky the rain and snow
Could we really let them go
Obviously the answer's no

Act now before it's too late
While we still have a world to appreciate
And don't let priorities diminish
To do so now will mean the finish
Because with polluted smog clouds hanging low across our land
Exit Homo Sapien a farewell goodbye to *man*.

Alan E Barlow

GRANDMA'S TEAPOTS

My grandma collects teapots
Though she hates the taste of tea
The last time that she counted them
They numbered ninety three
Displaying them upon her shelves
She talks of them with pride
Ignoring the remarks from relatives
Meant to deride
Every teapot holds a tale
Of where and how obtained
Each one to her a treasure
To be carefully maintained
Her favourites are placed
Inside a cabinet of glass
To be gazed upon admiringly
Each time she shuffles past
I love to see excitement
Set her wrinkled face aglow
When with packaged teapot to present
To grandma I can go.

Kim Montia

UNTITLED

Kingfisher watches
wet and shining by the bole
sapphire flash of insects
silver in the water

leaf and petal tremble
branch and trunk
begin to shake, roots
clutch the earth

she shudders mountains rise
rivers flow
continents are drifting . . .

bright wings in bark did all this

I saw it by the river

David Whitmarsh

MUM

When I think of how a mum should be
I always think of you -
You've been the rock supporting me,
The light to guide me through.
You've been the one I turn to first
Whenever I've been down
The one who tries to make me smile,
And ease away my frown.
You've been the one to make me well
Whenever I've been ill,
The one who's always shown the way
And given me the will
To learn from all my past mistakes,
And know what's right from wrong -
To keep my pride, my head held high,
Be thoughtful and be strong.
My childhood memories and your love
Will stay for years to come,
And the future holds no fears for me
Because you are my mum.

E C Devenish

REALISATIONS

Words are uttered which say so much.
Heart and soul wait for the touch.
Pleasing promises of better days
It's all so clear; there are no *rays*

Futile gestures, playing a game.
Faith? Who will take the blame?
Trusting fool offers it all,
Suddenly so far to fall.

Closer, closer, friendship destroyed
Nothing left now; empty void.
Contradictions divert true course.
Selfish desire, no remorse!

Free of misery, free of pain?
Faces at night, visions in rain.
Eternity of tears. Hatred amid hope
Commitment fears; cannot cope

Cold breath that whispers lies.
Dark heart that weeps and sighs.
Shadows form that hide the truth
Realisations condemn my youth.

Ann-Marie Marler

WORLD PEACE

Why is there so much fighting,
Why is there so much pain,
Why can't all the world be friends,
Surely no-one wants the world to end,
Why can't people live in peace,
With understanding,
Instead of demanding,
Why won't people let life's troubled waters settle,
Instead of like a kettle,
Keep it on the boil,
When they know,
That they will end up,
With nothing for their trouble,
Nothing for their toil,
Why can't people of the world,
Live with devotion,
Instead of emotion,
Hatred and rage,
Like lions in a cage,
For we could all live,
Hand in glove,
And show some brotherly love,
So let's all live as friends,
Surely no-one wants the world to end,
So let us have some joy,
Instead of sorrow,
And build a new world tomorrow,
Let us build a new world in the sun,
And we will all join hands as one,
Then we could all become good friends,
And bring all wars to an end.

R Scott

PRECIOUS CHRISTMAS PHOTOGRAPHS

Standing by a dark bamboo chair with a photographic stare,
Stood Great Great Grandmother her long satin bustle in a flare,
Her white lace collar crossed over her chest,
And wide white lace cuffs, in 1914 this was her Sunday best,
Her crinoline swept out in a blue layered magnificent fan,
And her matching lace pouffé cap had red roses on.

Great Grandmother tapped the calendar on the wall,
Then stood my mother on a chair because she was so small,
Tomorrow will be your birthday, Dorothy dear,
It was 1914 and the beginning of the first world war,
Then riding down the cobbled lane to church,
In a pony and trap she hoped the horses would not lurch,

My father rode on a high wooden rocking horse,
In a velvet smock and tight plus-fours,
With a wide white ruffle collar under his chin,
And shining tight curls and a cheeky grin,

In 1937 there is a picture of me holding a white rabbit,
Wearing a white silk smocked dress and bare feet on the carpet,
My brother too sitting on a leather pouffé,
With Father's curls and shiny black buttoned shoes, in angelic array,

In 1956 there are wedding photos of glittering pearls and a head-dress
of lace,
Grey top hats, cream cravats, spats, red roses again, flinging open
each face,
Then in 1965 cuddling my first baby to my heart,
I remember his first woo at the Christmas tree while in Grandmother's
arms,
He too had a rocking horse, this time made of tin,
Smiling, showing two little bottom teeth while riding up and down on
the springs,

My father left me a photo, he was showing me a red rose,
Departing this life, he left it in his office drawer for me, lying there in
quite repose.

Pauline Mary Starr

FICTION?

Little or naught do we know about what's going
On around us; for so many things are not what
They seem to be! Thus within us there's a growing
Suspicion that so many among us are not
Earthlings! But aliens who have been, secretly,
Transported from somewhere out there in outer space;
That this world is being taken over, slowly
But surely, by an unknown and different race;
That, in fact, they are here right now in a great force!
Disguised as humans; are taking over humans . . .
Man flatly refuses to believe this, of course.
Typical! Self-hoodwinking being one of man's
Disguises when from aught he wants to run away!
Kids himself that UFOs are: *fakes, tommy rot,*
Rubbish! Which is the majority view. That they
Have no proof of this doesn't bother them one jot!
What's more! Man is wont to condemn, out of hand, aught
He fears or doesn't understand which, sad but true,
Has nigh on oft' been his overthrow; and has brought
Him to grief and *shamed* him! So let's hope and pray, too,
That if this world is to *house* an alien race . . .
It's better than the human race has proved to be.
Well, just look at this man-fouled earth . . . it's a *disgrace!*
Is a grave threat to life . . . far-reaching and deadly.
But then, many of man's deeds beggar description!
He's a menace who could the whole universe *blow!*
Alien-controlled man could be far from fiction!
So what? If that brings peace and cleans up here below.

Jackie Holroyd

EMOTIONS

If I didn't care it wouldn't matter,
If I hadn't loved I wouldn't care.
A year has passed and still the thoughts continue,
There was a hidden silence which leaves me in despair.

I didn't understand although I tried hard,
I tried hard but I couldn't find a way.
The words refused to answer your despairing,
The thoughts were there my mouth refused to say.

We hid ourselves behind a velvet curtain,
The curtain's softness hid our hearts from view.
We laughed together falsely in our sadness,
Deliberately I closed my mind dismissed the cue.

The shallow laughter hid our true emotions,
Our true emotions packed into a case.
Sometimes I left so quickly to avoid it,
My shame, my guilt, despair, gave quickening pace.

Your anger and your bitterness so obvious.
So obvious you wanted so much more.
I gave you of my time my love rejected,
But age and passing time we can't restore.

So long the end in coming now so near.
So near to death your own true spirit came.
You gently pushed my hand away to tell me
Your fight was won and now there was no blame.

Your caring gentle way was now returning,
Returning to assure me and forgive.
The peace you searched for here at last,
But with my pain I have to live.

Valerie Lummus

GIFT OF LOVE

You gave me gifts when I was small
a bike, a scooter, but that's not all
Patience, kindness honesty
these special gifts you gave to me
Each year you gave a holiday
with a sandy beach and sunny days
So many memories for me to treasure
the kind that will stay in my heart forever
Each passing year you gave me gifts
that I think the whole world of
But the most precious gift you gave me
it was the gift of love.

Dawn Wilson

THE POWER STATION

Do you ever wonder about the light,
That helps you read your book at night,
The music you listen to during the day,
Computer games you like to play,
TV you watch at the flick of a switch
All of these things our life enrich.

Do you ever wonder about the men,
Who work at, and run the power station.
Toiling for hours night and day,
Keeping the country at work and play,
Put in the pool, making a bid,
Supplying it to the National Grid.

Do you ever wonder how it's made,
This force of power, a lethal aid,
Boiler house hot with hissing steam,
The throb of turbines power unseen.
Forcing generators to go round and round,
Sending the power through lines above ground.

Do you ever wonder when things go wrong.
Sitting without electricity for so long.
Follow procedure they have to be quick,
We all know oil and water don't mix.
Turn on the seal oil, make sure it's water tight,
Drain the boiler, weld the pipe.

Do you ever wonder when laid in bed,
The electric alarm next to your head,
Electric blanket ensconcing your frame
While in the kitchen, it's a waiting game
Next morning, while sipping your tea! Take time,
To take a fresh look at the power line.

Blanche Middleton

NATURE'S MEDICINE

When your heart is feeling weary
And your mind is feeling low,
And you think, at every second
Life will bring another blow!

Take yourself to nature,
Let it heal your soul and heart,
Nature puts things in perspective,
Helps your troubles to depart!

In the winter, put your coat on
Walk out and close the door!
With the grass, or snow, your carpet
Lying soft upon the floor!

Breathe the air, so fresh and calming,
In the summer, smell the green,
The intoxicating flowers
Will make your heart serene!

The rain will wash your worries
And the sunshine warm your heart,
The wind will blow your cares away
And, the birdsong plays its part!

Put your trust in Mother Nature,
She will comfort you and guide,
Help make your journey into life
A far less bumpy ride!

Shirley Williamson

ROSES IN AUTUMN

Bushes of beautiful roses bloom
  Adorning the gardens again,
    Displaying exquisite beauty
      Defying the wind and the rain.

From the very depths of their growth
  To the end of each delicate branch,
    Various coloured velvet roses grow
      Which the odd breeze coaxes to dance.

Sending sweet aromas floating
  Through the cool autumn air,
    Petals spiralling down to the ground
      As seasonal memories we share.

So, as autumn wends on to winter,
  Those beautiful roses will die,
    Such pleasure through the year they give.
      Roll on next summer I sigh.

Joan A Anscombe

MY FRIENDS

My first friend was leggy,
With wrinkled socks and laced shoes.
Her plaits were unruly about her freckled face.
The hop, skip and jump?
A game that we always played.
My secondary school friend
Was quiet and just so,
Her shoes shone like conkers,
And so did her hair.
Our headmistress had a steely glare!
My next friend was huge,
And, let's be fair.
We both filled our maternity wear
'Life begins at forty'
My older friend would say
When I look back on the years,
Seems not more than just a day.

Mary E Wain

WARM THOUGHTS

The wind blows harsh and cold,
As winter starts to unfold.
Bring rain and sleet,
Fog and ice,
Dark grey days and stormy nights.
To bed tonight I will go,
Tucked up warm from frost and snow.
And dream of spring's awakening,
With welcome warmth and colours so gay,
Bees and butterflies back to play.
If I could I'd sleep till spring,
And awake together with all the delights,
I know it will bring.

M Murphy

WHAT'S A POEM?

Words!
- Mere choice or chance?
Made to enhance belief in man's creative art,
Veiled musings' better part.
Virtuoso and essential start - the best words ordered well
Their true import to tell.
Ecstatic intuition; imagining's rendition;
Fecundity; conceived idea; the God given.
Inspiration's elevation; a craft well riven;
Divinity's sorority, erudition and simplicity.

But stay - a poem must be
Words said with care, not just a litany;
Utterances of earth and air, not mere cacophony.
Synchromatic sounds, a myriad things
Speaking as torrents, stars or just lapwings.
Signified as Sapphics or ritualised Phillippics;
Mediumship;
Syntactical midwifery, lexical loquacity, rhapsodic metricality,
Where lies the shift in wordy thrift?
'Tis but a gift.

Robert Coburn

NORMA

She was gentle she was shy.
Eyes cast down as boys walked by.
She was young with worldly ways,
Played the mum in her early days.

Upon her brow the worried frown
Washing and cleaning would get her down
A mother child she did her best
As through the war we came with zest.

She was quiet, she was calm
Not many coins to grease her palm
She never worked to earn her bread
She just cared for us instead.

As oft these memories I recall
The elfin face the most of all
She had no desire to wed.
She just cared for us instead.

G Morris

AUTUMN

The rook's nest stands abandoned, in a tree bereft of life.
A tree left bare - prepared for winter's pending strife.
Shadows everywhere, from a cold, pale yellow distant light.

Seagulls and mallards, repose on a nearby frozen lake.
Rabbits in their burrow. Foxes in their lair.
One solitary magpie. Stands, stares and ponders on its fate.

Once green reeds, now broken and dark brown, lean and bend towards
the fast beckoning stream.
Linnets in the hedgerow - light brown, with a tint of white.
A blue white clouded sky, meets this sightly autumn land.
In a cold pale yellow light - from a distant sun, no longer bright.

Harry Glover

A COUNTRY WARDEN

Every day, I wake to see,
One more leaf, upon the tree.
Another day, another dawn.
The countryside, in early morn.
There's no-one else, but me about,
To stand and watch each leaf, come out.

Translucent clouds, cast ribbons of light.
Turn fields, and hills, to golden bright.
Weightless as cotton, on the breeze.
The warm wind, whispers through the trees.
Nothing gives me greater pleasure,
Than to walk the countryside, I treasure.

Irene Costello

LOST!

'Lost! Damn, where did it go?
I blinked, and I was looking forward so much.'

I think I know who took it -
But not where it went. It went,
Bit by bit, and I did not care,
- until now.

In those days of joy as a little boy,
It mattered so little, I was invincible,
And eternal life was before me, (with little behind).
Colours were clear and pure, and the sun always shone.
My world and I were both so very young.

Today it rained. Winter has come too soon.
In the silence I wander far, through seas of time.
Once friendly and warm, now cold and deep, and unknown to me.
Pictures of that time have faded, the paint has peeled.
Memories are mirrors, with jagged cracks.

'So, it was Time, my rival for years.
He took the past, leaving no stain but tears.'
(And still he is not satisfied!)

C M Wilkinson

OLD FRIENDS

There's Beatrice and Kathleen
old friends of mine, known them
for ages but no valentine.

Even my sister I cannot trace
and the going is still apace.

In the meantime happy days, good
wishes to you all
and let's have a ball.

Albert Usher

FIRST ANNIVERSARY

Twelve months have passed
but the pain still lasts.
For seasons may have changed
but memories remain the same.
And wishes are still
in the air.
Words may be spoken
and kindness shown.
But the void still remains
in one's soul.
Time moves on -
with no give or take.
But the flame of memories
lives on.
Some with tears,
others with a smile.
So we are brought together,
caught - in a moment of time.

Sandra E Kirton

LIFE'S REAL TREASURES

Walking in the countryside,
fills my heart full of pride,
the beauty that is ours to see,
is here for you as well as me.

I watch a squirrel scamper by,
bushy tail and bright eye,
he dropped an acorn from a tree,
it landed on the floor by me.

A rabbit in a nearby field,
darts away as I walk by,
down his burrow on the ground,
where he feels safe and sound.

I can hear the birds' sweet songs,
as the leaves begin to fall,
Robin redbreast watches me,
from his perch upon the wall.

Coloured leaves beneath my feet,
like a carpet made of gold,
in ambers, yellows, reds and greens,
there's a story to be told.

Nature's treasures all on show,
as the seasons come and go,
each one different in its own way,
as they change from day to day.

S J Hill

A THOUGHT ON ARMISTICE DAY

Owls' silent wings herald death proportionate,
Small mouse - demise unfortunate.
In human sphere our passing comes with noise corrosive,
With guns and cannon - and explosive.

P J Ball

ODE TO A VAMPIRE

I fear you with my soul yet I don't know what
you are,
You haunt the night, I sense you in the air;
You await my surrender, your voice constantly
utters my name.

I feel your presence behind me, your fingers
trace my spine.
I want you, yet detest you;
Your spirit haunts me by both day and night.
You fill my thoughts and torment my dreams,
Sleep is no refuge from your bewitching gaze.

Around every corner you seem to hide,
Endlessly watching me, waiting.
Wherever I run to, you follow;
Nowhere harbours me from your satanic grin.

Your perseverance finally weakens me,
I sense my resistance diminishing.
Having no longer strength to flee from you,
No more places in which to shelter,
Crumpled I fall, my will finally defeated.
I await your arrival,
I am ready to yield to your desires.

Lindsay Ellis

HERON

Motionless 'nd standing, shadow 'neath the trees,
Heron, can you see him, twixt water 'nd the reeds.
Patiently he waits, grey statue quiet pool,
Spearman by a water's edge, beak a butcher's tool.

See him strike grey lightning, silver pierced right through,
Flick, 'nd then he swallows, heron never chew.
Patiently 'nd standing, silent by the reeds,
Spearman 'nd a butcher, see the heron feeds.

Angled legs not streamlined, see him now in flight,
More a plastic sack, than a great red kite.
Flying ever higher, wings quite out of synch,
Modern pterodactyl, heron missing link.

Ivan Langham

DTC THE WAY TO BE

The way to psychuous pleasures
Is discipline, thought and control
To know right from wrong all the time
Then your life shall be on a roll

Psychuous means to try
To be happy in every way
Earning loadsamoney
More than the bills you must pay

A loving wife or husband
And kids with all they want
Governments out of power
In a few years time we want

So now you all shall know
How to eliminate
All that is bad in this world
And make yourself great

H G Griffiths

MONEY MAN ALL GONE

Look at the fool talking to himself
Doesn't he know people are laughing at him.
Why doesn't he turn and hold our eyes?
Whenever he speaks, he looks to the ground.

Along time ago he married a woman
Beautiful, stunning, sly like a fox
She took his love and all she could
Then let him down, like a lead balloon.

She took him to church and took all his money,
She got pregnant and then took his child,
She got the divorce and took all his happiness,
She took everything and got at his pride.

Where is his pride, his upright nature,
His great social standing, his circle of friends,
All have gone, along with his money,
His friends like leeches have sucked him dry.

The poor little fool has been trussed like a chicken
Tied and bound, gagged and restrained,
Left with nothing but expanses of pain,
His money, his friends, his home's all gone.

Matthew Collins

NON-COMMUNICATION

Our world with all advances made *super highways*
Spaceships, communication data fed into your head
Spoilt for choice our children play Nintendo games
Video films, computer info, washed down with tea and jam and bread

Parents yelling go away, watch the telly - go and play?

Communication a thing of the past, favourite games
No longer last, *snakes and ladders, ludo* too, old
Fashioned play that once you knew.

Now solitary games are all you know *one in one*
Eyes scanning hard nothing to say you concentrate each day
Parents now pleased to see you quiet, sit and watch their
TV prison no more speech just watching visions.

'Time for bed' is finally heard, this family who have
Sat all night without a word.

Gill Sandy

I'M ASKING YOU NOW

There's a spark in your eye,
I'm asking myself why,
Is it because you're in love.
There's a ring in your voice,
Have you fallen in love,
Are you making a choice,
Oh, heavens above.
I'm asking you now will you tell me true,
That you love me as I love you.
Forever we'll be in a world of our own,
Reaping together the seeds we have sown.
I'm asking you dear have I read the signs well,
Do you love me, I never can tell.
At the end of the day what will you say,
To the question I'm asking you now.
Tell me you love me, as I love you true,
Of course, my darling, you give me your vow,
I'll always love and cherish you now.
So let's be together, I love you forever,
All of me darling, I give to you.
My questions are answered, content I will be,
Living and loving how happy we'll be.

Alice Stapleton

HAND OF DEATH

The hand of death
Touches shoulders bare
You turn around
And there is no-one there
Your time on earth is fading
Your gaze in wonder stares
Breathing starts to grip the throat
Then motionless declared
The hand of time
Has stopped the key
That kept the heart
That beat for thee.

Brenda Walton

LOVE

Love is not infatuation,
Or merely just a fling.
Not even when the first kiss is snatched going round the maypole ring.
Love grows within us, which comes with respect,
The bond grows stronger which comes from within.
Love is sharing, always caring for the person we are attracted to.
This in turn gives a feeling of pride surging up from inside,
Which is so difficult to hide.
We find ourselves hoping very strongly that same person
Will also find this feeling difficult to hide.

Ena Pullen

MY ONLY SON

I have to leave today my little son
Your mum and I can't live together any more
You're too young to understand
I have done everything I can to stay with you,
Your photographs I'll carry
I'll carry on my heart.
You're young someday you will grow up
to be a man.
Then I'll tell you all I can
and you will understand,
I will keep in touch with you
I never will forget you,
Even though you're only 9
time will fly.
When you grow up you can
make up your own mind
I'll be far across the sea
I'll want you to come and live with me.
And we will be happy once again
time will pass so quickly
the tears are in my eyes
so I'll say goodbye to you
          my son.

Jean McCool

A DAY IN THE LIFE . . .
OF A CONSERVATIVE MP - AN HONEST ACCOUNT

Sitting in the kitchen with tea and toast,
The letter box rattles, it's the morning post,
The saved letters are from my directorships,
The ones from constituents are in the bin,
I pay attention to those from businesses
Offering money for questions to the House,
I don't think this is a sin,
Being an MP working 14 hours a day is a
hard and busy life,
With business concerns, parliament,
three mistresses and a wife,
The morning is spent on business in London,
lunch is spent drinking free sherry in the
parliamentary bar,
Accepting money from lobbyists, it will buy
me another new car,
Life's a party and three cheers for John Major,
Who means a lot to me,
Because thanks to him I am here where
I can make speeches and pretend to be sincere,
The afternoon is spent in a compulsory debate,
It's three hours sleep, after shouting for my
Side and booing at the opposition,
Who are only jealous 'cause they are not in
my position,
Will they never learn how to cheat properly
like I did at public school,
In which cheating was encoded in every single
rule,
Then I vote in the aye (yes) lobby, I
haven't a clue what for,

But who cares anyway as long as I can
get more,
It's 7pm and oh what an exhausting day,
But I'm 3 million richer, so I guess I
did OK.

Emma Kemm

LIFE IN LEICESTERSHIRE

Here I am in glorious Leicestershire
In Charnwood, with the birds flying high and all the wild flowers here
Walking in Bradgate Park and feeding the ducks and watching the deer.
The peace and the beauty of Leicestershire it is all here.
How lucky am I to be able to see
All the beauty and peace of the countryside around me.
As I sit with my thoughts, under this old oak tree,
Looking back in time, did famous Jane Grey sit here, like me.
Enjoying the park, her thoughts wandering,
To London, and Henry the king.
What stories abound, as I look around.
The brook babbling by, with the fish swimming happily by.
The ducks splashing about, the children laughing and shout.
The kites are flying up high, in the sky.
And you can hear the wind in the trees sigh.
All the love and happiness was here, and at this moment of time is here.
And in the future years will still be here, in glorious Leicestershire.

Doreen O'Brien

TWO INTO ONE, ONE INTO TWO

Autumnal break shall I get a window seat
or next to aisle space for awkward feet,
who will share this final trip with me
motorway services sip inflated tea.
Close to the window small and neat
in a purse his photograph she keeps;
power-stations, bridged rivers, traversing moors
do you often travel these short-break tours,
high green coach gliding to destruction
long vehicles mile after mile slow lane seduction
life's been hard since my good Earnest went
died on pilgrimage to Canterbury, Kent,
my daughter, grand children a great god-send
without them by loss driven round the bend.
are you a non-smoker I sincerely hope so
for repairs two lanes closed, one way slow.
single room tunnelled traffic drums beyond
she no longer bimbo, I of her grown fond;
casual breakfast served formal dinner
half-board fading non-repentant sinner,
we're in the lord's hands I believe you know
forced words maintain conversational flow,
photographed together her two friends as well
Bede's holy place tolled prayers a single bell,
a melancholic regret to all true desire
arm around her waist to her room retire,
feeder-point bus-station end of break
exchange address two who loved forever separate.

David Crossland

THE BEACH

There are some lovely shells at the beach,
Some quite near, some out of reach.
The waves lap at the golden sand,
Then it trickles through my hand.
We always buy a cold ice cream,
It tastes like we're in a dream.
You can make pictures in the sand
Then walk along the pier and listen to the band.

Katy Briggs

INFORMATION

We hope you have enjoyed reading this book - and that you will continue to enjoy it in the coming years.

If you like reading and writing poetry drop us a line, or give us a call, and we'll send you a free information pack.

Write to :-
Anchor Books Information
1-2 Wainman Road
Woodston
Peterborough
PE2 7BU
(01733) 230761

CONTENTS

FOREWORD

Anchor Books is a small press, established in 1992, with the aim of promoting readable poetry to as wide an audience as possible.

We hope to establish an outlet for writers of poetry who may have struggled to see their work in print.

The poems presented here have been selected from many entries. Editing proved to be a difficult task and as the Editor, the final selection was mine.

Poetic Words From The East is a fine collection of poetry which has been contributed from poets from this particular area.

The poets delve deep into their emotions to express through their 'poetic words' how they feel about everyday issues which concern them. The poems reflect their opinions on today's society, the style and theme is varied throughout the anthology.

Most of all poets are united in their passion for poetry, and I trust will be a riveting read by young and old alike, and will leave you delighted by its content for years to come.

I trust this selection will delight and please the authors and all those who enjoy reading poetry.

Heather Killingray
Editor

First published in Great Britain in 1997 by
ANCHOR BOOKS
1-2 Wainman Road, Woodston,
Peterborough, PE2 7BU
Telephone (01733) 230761

HB ISBN 1 85930 488 5
SB ISBN 1 85930 483 4

ANCHOR BOOKS

POETIC WORDS FROM THE EAST

Edited by

Heather Killingray